WICCA

ELEMENTAL MAGIC

MAGIC

A Guide to the Elements, Witchcraft, and Magic Spells

LISA CHAMBERLAIN

Wicca Elemental Magic

Copyright © 2014 by Lisa Chamberlain.

Published by **Chamberlain Publications (Wicca Shorts)**

ISBN-13: 978-1-912715-66-4

Disclaimer

No part of this publication may be reproduced or transmitted in any form or by any means, mechanical or electronic, including photocopying or recording, or by any information storage and retrieval system, or transmitted by email without permission in writing from the publisher.

While all attempts have been made to verify the information provided in this publication, neither the author nor the publisher assumes any responsibility for errors, omissions, or contrary interpretations of the subject matter herein.

This book is for entertainment purposes only. The views expressed are those of the author alone, and should not be taken as expert instruction or commands. The reader is responsible for his or her own actions.

Adherence to all applicable laws and regulations, including international, federal, state, and local governing professional licensing, business practices, advertising, and all other aspects of doing business in the US, Canada, or any other jurisdiction is the sole responsibility of the purchaser or reader.

Neither the author nor the publisher assumes any responsibility or liability whatsoever on the behalf of the purchaser or reader of these materials.

Any perceived slight of any individual or organization is purely unintentional.

YOUR FREE GIFT

Thank you for adding this book to your Wiccan library! To learn more, why not join Lisa's Wiccan community and get an exclusive, free spell book?

The book is a great starting point for anyone looking to try their hand at practicing magic. The ten beginner-friendly spells can help you to create a positive atmosphere within your home, protect yourself from negativity, and attract love, health, and prosperity.

Little Book of Spells is now available to read on your laptop, phone, tablet, Kindle or Nook device!

To download, simply visit the following link:

www.wiccaliving.com/bonus

GET THREE
FREE AUDIOBOOKS
FROM LISA CHAMBERLAIN

Did you know that all of Lisa's books are available in audiobook format? Best of all, you can get **three audiobooks completely free** as part of a 30-day trial with Audible.

Wicca Starter Kit contains three of Lisa's most popular books for beginning Wiccans, all in one convenient place. It's the best and easiest way to learn more about Wicca while also taking audiobooks for a spin! Simply visit:

www.wiccaliving.com/free-wiccan-audiobooks

Alternatively, *Spellbook Starter Kit* is the ideal option for building your magical repertoire using candle and color magic, crystals and mineral stones, and magical herbs. Three spellbooks —over 150 spells—are available in one free volume, here:

www.wiccaliving.com/free-spell-audiobooks

Audible members receive free audiobooks every month, as well as exclusive discounts. It's a great way to experiment and see if audiobook learning works for you.

If you're not satisfied, you can cancel anytime within the trial period. You won't be charged, and you can still keep your books!

CONTENTS

INTRODUCTION

What do magical spells, wishing wells, rain dances, and lucky rabbit's feet have in common? All of these customs are rooted in the idea that unseen forces can have an influence on the occurrences of our daily lives.

Even in this modern age of science and "reason," people still give at least some credence to superstitions: we cross our fingers and knock on wood for luck, and we avoid walking under ladders to prevent bad luck.

Whether we are conscious of it or not, all of these ideas and traditions are tied to underlying properties of the energy that makes up the entire Universe. This energy is found in everything on Earth, visible and invisible, including every human being. This energy is particularly essential to Witchcraft, and is the main focus of this book.

As interest in Wicca and other forms of Witchcraft continues to grow, interested readers will find a vast array of information about the Craft and its rich, varied beliefs and traditions. From coven-oriented, highly structured forms of Wicca to looser, eclectic and solitary forms of practice, people from all across the spectrum are sharing their knowledge with those who feel pulled in the direction of what many call "The Old Religion."

Terminology across these sources will vary, with some authors distinguishing between "Wicca" and "Witchcraft," and some making no distinction at all. This is just the way it is with Wicca: with no sacred text to study, many Wiccans end up taking their own, often very unique, journey as they discover the religion for themselves. This means that two authors can write on the same topic from completely different perspectives—it all depends on the author's personal beliefs, knowledge, and experiences.

With this in mind, there is no right or wrong, and this partly explains why there are so many differing—and on occasion, conflicting—opinions to be heard. For example, some Wiccans will practice Witchcraft actively, as part of their daily lives; however, other Wiccans will *never* participate in Witchcraft, and disassociate from it completely. Both are perfectly valid approaches—my advice to you is to take in as much information as possible, and then form your own set of beliefs based on the ideas and practices that resonate most with you.

This particular book offers a view of Wiccan-oriented ritual and magic through the lens of the Elements—Earth, Air, Fire and Water, as well as Spirit, the Fifth Element—and is intended for beginners and more seasoned Witches alike.

For thousands of years, the Elements have been considered the basic building blocks of the Universe, and they are inherent to the basic principles of Witchcraft. Wiccans and other Witches recognize, honor and participate with these core energies in both religious ritual and magic. By attuning to and working with the magical qualities of the Elements, both individually and combined, Witches are able to manifest positive changes for themselves and others, fostering a deeper spiritual connection to the natural world.

One way of tuning in to that connection is through an understanding of the principle of *animism*, which is a major concept this guide to Elemental magic will discuss.

A concept that has spanned the cultures of the globe for millennia, animism takes for granted that there is more to the material world than we can grasp with our usual five senses. Some Witches have also always taken this for granted, but many have to study and practice for awhile before finding themselves grounded in what is for them, coming from contemporary culture, a new reality.

This is where getting to know the Elements on a more intimate level can be very helpful.

This book will introduce you to each of the Elements: their properties, characteristics, and their use in magic. You'll learn how the Elements are invoked in ritual, as well as some techniques and magical practices for working with individual Elements.

This book is by no means an exhaustive source of information, and the ideas it presents should never be considered the "way things are always done," but should instead provide you with a springboard to make your own discoveries about the power of the Elements and the magic they have to offer.

Blessed Be.

PART ONE

INTRODUCTION TO THE ELEMENTS

ELEMENTS AND THE LIVING UNIVERSE

What do the Elements have to do with our modern way of life?

Particularly in the developed countries of the West, it may seem that the answer is "*not much*." Apart from weather events that can cause major inconveniences and the occasional catastrophe, we live life relatively removed from the basic forces of nature.

Even if we rarely think about it on a conscious level, we all understand how important the four Elements—Earth, Air, Fire, and Water—are for our survival. We need air to breathe, of course, and water to sustain life. We live on the Earth and depend on it as a source of food for sustenance, and fire—in the form of light, heat, and energy—is quite essential.

However, despite acknowledging their fundamental importance, most of us remain incredibly detached from the Elements.

We no longer have to build fires to heat our homes during the cold Winter months, and we can even keep out the sweltering Summer air with insulation. We have no need to worry about sourcing water, which is as easy as turning on a tap. Furthermore, most of us are very far removed from the sources of our food, and there's an enormous variety of "food" products on grocery store shelves with ingredients that do even not come naturally from the Earth.

It almost seems as if we've gone to great lengths in the "civilized world" to get as far away from the Elements as possible. After all, they can be detrimental to our health and safety in many ways, as we can see in the phrase "exposure to the elements," which is often used in the context of damage or death.

What Witches know is that the Elements are powerful forces in their own right, with benevolent as well as destructive properties. They are necessary for the functioning of all life, even though they can be dangerous.

The Elements are perhaps the ultimate expression of the co-creative nature of the Universe, as each interacts with all others in the physical realm, and each participates in its own way in the ongoing cycles of life and death. These forces are a fundamental part of Wicca and other nature-based religions, and they can, with practice and intention, be directed to cause a desired change in our lives—in fact, this is the essence of what magic and spellwork is.

But how do the Elements *work* in Witchcraft?

There are a number of ways to answer this, and different answers will come from different books, traditions, and individual practitioners. But a brief look at the lineage of Wiccan beliefs can help illuminate the general concepts that underlie the magic of the Elements.

ANCIENT CULTURES AND THE NATURAL WORLD

While Wicca as a religion has quite modern origins, its beliefs and practices borrow from many older sources, including deities from ancient Egypt, India, Greece and Rome; holidays from old European pagan traditions; and magical lore from the Celtic world.

A key element of many of these older traditions is what anthropologists call *animism*. This term refers to a worldview that is very different from the mainstream worldview of most modern Western cultures.

Over the past few centuries, conventional science has shaped the modern perspective that the material world is *only* material, with no connection to the spiritual world (if, in fact, the spiritual world is even recognized at all). For those who don't believe in a spiritual world, the separation is seen as between mind and matter, an idea made popular by the philosopher Descartes in the 17th century.

The animistic perspective, by contrast, is that there is *no separation at all* between the material and spiritual worlds, and this belief underlies much of the work of Witchcraft.

The word "animism" is derived from the Latin *animus*, which means "soul" or "mind." In this orientation to the world, the quality of soul, or spirit, is not limited to humans or even all living creatures, but is found in all things.

Many animistic cultures view certain objects in the natural world—such as trees and other plants, springs and other bodies of water, and various geological formations—as having individual souls, or holding particularly strong spirit energy. These objects may be considered sacred to particular deities, or physical manifestations of unnamed spirits.

For example, in Greek mythology, humans were often transformed into trees and other plant life, where their spirits remained. Greek and Latin mythologies abound with various types of nymphs—

female spirits who inhabit particular land forms, including trees and mountains, as well as bodies of water, the sky, and the Underworld. The Mayans are known to have prayed to the spirits of weather phenomena, such as clouds and lightning. And ancient goddesses and gods of Egypt were invoked into amulets and talismans worn for help with fertility, hunting, and other aspects of successful living.

In other words, the majority of ancient religions embraced animism, at least to some extent. As a result, animism is often said to be the fundamental basis from which later religions grew.

Now, for our hunter-gatherer ancestors, the relationship with nature was much more direct and intimate than it is for us today. While many of us may seek experience with the natural world through camping trips or long hikes, our ancestors lived their entire lives in "the great outdoors," where there really was no "material world" to stand in the way of communing with the spiritual—there was none of the noise of our modern world to drown out nature's messages. Instead, being in tune with the life force in all things was simply part of the human experience.

It is said that as hunter-gatherer societies gradually gave over to agriculturally based societies, animism became more elaborate, giving rise to deities who became responsible for particular aspects of the physical world. There are gods who rule over types of weather, as well as gods associated with human activity such as war, hunting, and the harvest. Some deities were assigned to the spiritual world, as well—such as **Hades, who rules the Greek Underworld, and Arawn, the king of the Welsh Otherworld.**

Although the rise of Christianity and Islam all but stamped out ancient religions in many parts of the world, animism has survived into modern times in various places.

In parts of Indonesia, where traditional indigenous cultural practices have been officially "outlawed," people still believe in the spirits of natural phenomena like trees and rocks, as well as rice, which is considered to have a soul similar to that of humans, and is grown and tended to with ceremonial rituals to ensure abundance.

In many Native American traditions, animals are an integral part of spiritual growth for those who walk the animist path. Alternately called animal totems or power animals, they serve as teachers, guides, and messengers for people on their journey through life.

Native American medicine also incorporates animism, as the sacred herbs involved in traditional healing are considered to have spirits themselves. These plants are treated with the utmost respect and are prayed to and thanked before they are picked for use in ritual. Some healers even have the ability to "hear" the plant spirits and thus learn their potential uses directly from the plant. This is how many indigenous peoples learned to use herbal medicine in the first place.

In Ireland, people still tie ribbons or strips of cloth to hawthorn trees, known as "wishing trees," as a form of prayer. Ancient springs and wells, whose waters are believed to contain the powers of the Otherworld, are found all across the Celtic Isles. These places were later renamed "holy wells" as Christianity merged with the indigenous **Celtic religion.**

The Irish landscape is also dotted with several enchanted places, which are often hills or ancient religious sites, where an invisible population of spirits, or "sidhe" (pronounced "shee") are said to live. The sidhe were the people who inhabited Ireland before the coming of the Celts, who "walked into the Earth" rather than surrender to their conquerors. Their dwellings are often called fairy forts or fairy mounds, and there are even places known as "fairy paths," where it's considered unwise to build homes or undertake any other construction.

Animism is a very general term—not a religion in and of itself, but a way of classifying religions and belief systems that are not monotheistic like most of today's major world religions. Each animistic tradition is unique to its own culture, and people in these cultures would not call themselves "animistic," since this is a Western term used to describe them from the outside.

From the inside, there is no need to have a term. It is taken for granted that the world is alive and full of spirits who are as connected with human life as the air itself, and that the energies of these spirits can be called on to help with the practical realities of daily life.

Witchcraft makes particular use of this last idea: that we can consciously communicate with the spiritual world and manifest positive changes in our circumstances, both on a personal level and for others.

Witches may do this largely through working with their own chosen deities, whether these deities have specific identities (such as Flora, the Roman goddess of flowers, or Cernunnos, the Irish god of wild animals) or are simply recognized as the Goddess and the God: the female and male creative energies that power the life cycles we witness on Earth year after year.

Some Witches may not actually believe in any deities *per se*, but instead commune with the spirits of the natural world as they understand them on an individual level. Some may even focus their spiritual and magical work simply through communing with the one force believed to be inherent throughout the Universe. They may call this force "the Universe," "the Spirit," "All That Is," or any other term that best describes their experience of these energies.

Most Wiccans and Witches, however, devote some degree of specific attention to the Elements in their practice, with a definite awareness of the spiritual presence inherent in each of these forces of nature.

MODERN OBSERVATIONS OF THE NATURAL WORLD

Interestingly, some discoveries in the scientific fields seem to support aspects of the animistic perspective.

For example, it was demonstrated in the late 19th century by physicists Pierre and Jaques Currie that certain crystals, such as quartz and tourmaline, are piezoelectric. This means they can generate an electric charge when mechanical stress is applied, such as tapping them with a hammer. Some crystals also exhibit a pyroelectric effect, releasing an electric charge when exposed to a temperature change.

While these phenomena can be illustrated and described in purely "mechanical" terms, they also seem to point to a larger reality of crystals—that they are "alive" and participating in the ongoing creative force of the Universe in ways we can't see with the naked eye.

The practice of using crystals for emotional and physical healing, which dates back to ancient times and has seen a resurgence in recent decades, is rooted in this idea, and while their effectiveness has yet to be demonstrated by traditional scientific methods, there is plenty of testimony among users of these alternative healing modalities.

Another seeming convergence between scientific thought and the animistic paradigm is found in our evolving understanding of plant biology.

In the 1970s, a book called *The Secret Life of Plants*, by Peter Tompkins and Christopher Bird, described various experiments involving plants connected to polygraph machines. The machines registered the plants' apparent responses to the thoughts of people nearby, as well as to destructive behavior, such as stomping on another plant, an event that was apparently remembered by the plant "witness" after the fact. The book was widely discredited as "pseudo-science," but it helped promote the idea that plants are somehow influenced by external stimuli that would seem to have no logical effect on their behavior.

In the 21st century, some researchers are arguing that plants actually exhibit intelligence in various ways. For example, in one recent experiment, a plant exposed to a recording of a caterpillar chewing on a leaf produced chemicals used to defend against attack. In another, plants roots were observed to grow toward a buried pipe that was dry on the outside, but contained flowing water. Plants have at least three times the number of distinct senses as human beings, which enable them to sense and respond to everything in their environments, including chemicals in the air, different wavelengths of light, and other plant life in their vicinity.

One of the more fascinating discoveries has been the networks of "information exchange" observed in forests.

Scientists have been able to track the flow of nutrients and chemical signals exchanged along pathways through a "web" of fungi living underground. These studies have shown that older trees will share nutrients with younger trees that are still too shaded to get enough sunlight on their own, and that trees of one species will actually "cooperate" with other species by trading nutrients back and forth at different points in the growing season.

There has been intense debate among researchers in the plant sciences regarding the word "intelligence" as applied to plant life. Many scientists associate this word strictly with animals, and prefer terms like "electrical signaling" to anything that might suggest neurological activity, even though neurotransmitter chemicals such as dopamine and serotonin have been found in plants. But this is really an argument over the traditional scientific classifications of living organisms. The observed behavior of the plants themselves is not in dispute, and it offers an unprecedented glimpse into the invisible realms of the "inanimate" world.

Finally, there has been much interest in recent years in the work and publications of Dr. Masaro Emoto, a Japanese social scientist who turned his attention in the 1990s to the study of water.

Starting with the knowledge that no two snowflakes are identical, Emoto sought to find a way to view the molecular structure of water by freezing small samples of water from various sources, and then viewing it under a microscope as it began to thaw. After some trial and error, he was successful—hexagonal crystals emerged under the microscope, expanding three dimensionally as the water began to thaw, and then disappearing as the water returned to liquid form.

Emoto then began to experiment by using different stimuli on the water before freezing it, to see whether the appearance of the crystals would be affected. In particular, he tried exposing the water samples to visual images, verbal and written messages in various languages, as well as music and prayer.

The results he shared were astounding to many: water which had been subjected to positive messages and prayer formed more complete, aesthetically pleasing crystals, while water which had been exposed to negative messaging and negative emotions produced less complete and misshapen crystals.

Emoto documented these experiments with photographs that were published in a series of books called *Messages From Water*, along with his interpretations of the results: that water responds to the energetic charge of words, thoughts, emotions, and even art forms. Since water makes up around 70% of the human body, the implications for our own well-being when it comes to thoughts and feelings are important.

Another significant finding was that the source of the water being examined made a difference—water from more pristine sources, such as a waterfall in rural Japan, produced higher-quality crystals and with more consistency than tap water from urban sources, which tended not to produce any at all.

Emoto described the phenomena he observed in the context of his theory of "Hado," a term based on the Japanese ideograms for both "move" and "wave." Hado is essentially the subatomic vibrational quality of all matter in the Universe. It can be thought of as similar to "chi," but Hado as a concept is more centered on the relationship between human consciousness and the rest of existence.

The theory of Hado recognizes that thoughts and feelings are physical matter, and that changing our own vibrational energy can change the material world. Using this concept, Emoto and a few hundred of his supporters performed a prayer healing of a large, polluted lake in West Japan that resulted in significant reduction of the algae and odor that have plagued the lake every summer for decades. Emoto has used his discoveries to promote the importance of taking care of our water as a global resource.

Of course, conventional science has dismissed Emoto's work due to its lack of sufficient adherence to the scientific method. Emoto doesn't claim that his work meets these standards, but the results have been astounding enough to defy any "rational" explanation that the scientific model can currently offer. But in the realm of quantum physics, the theory of Hado doesn't appear to be so far-fetched.

It has parallels with ideas in newer, more cutting-edge scientific theories that also recognize the vibrational nature of matter and describe the most fundamental "building block" of matter as being, essentially, information, or "mental energy."

One physicist, Nick Herbert, has argued that mind permeates all of reality, and actually uses the term "quantum animism" to describe this fundamental quality of the Universe. Indeed, it seems that Descartes' conviction that mind is separate from matter, which has been so entrenched in Western scientific thought, is now being turned on its head.

ANIMISM, THE ELEMENTS, AND WITCHCRAFT

Of course, Witches don't need scientific proof of the animistic nature of the Universe in order to know that it is at work in all aspects of life.

They learn from their own experiments how to communicate with crystals, plants and water, as well as air and fire. The Craft is about revering nature in all its forms, and harnessing the vibrational power of *All That Is* to create positive change.

Working with a particular crystal, for example, Witches might hold the stone in both hands for a few moments and attune with its energies. Many people—not just Witches, Wiccans, and Pagans—have experienced differing sensations from holding different types of crystals in healing and spiritual work. Some crystals, like pyrite, can feel very energetic and "buzzy," while others, like moss agate, have a calming effect.

In addition to physical, spiritual and emotional healing, these Earth energies provide pathways to magical change. Pyrite, for example, is often used in magical work for self-confidence and wealth. Moss agate protects the aura from negative energy.

Water is traditionally part of every Wiccan ritual, either physically present or symbolically represented by a cup, a chalice, or a cauldron.

The water can even be a focus of the ritual, charged with the Witch's personal power for a particular intention. Some spells involve magical drinking water, charged with the energies of crystals or herbs. Water is also a scrying tool—Witches can gaze at the surface of a cauldron of water for images that communicate information from the unseen realms.

Air, being invisible, seems to be a much less tangible Element, but it often makes its presence known nonetheless. Sometimes it's subtle, and sometimes it's impossible to ignore.

Poets and Witches alike have invoked the wind and recognized its "personalities," from gentle to fierce, and it's not an uncommon thing to feel a particular "energy" in the air, especially just before a good storm. Wind works very symbiotically with the four directions, and the particular direction the wind is coming from at a given time can be more useful for particular magical work. For example, Western winds are good for strengthening intuition.

Fire is perhaps the Element most often associated with Witchcraft in the popular imagination. This could be because the spirit of fire is so easy to observe, as flames appear to dance on the wick or in the hearth.

Candles are widely used in ritual, and often are a key part of magical work. Outdoor rituals may make use of bonfires, which become very powerful tools of transformation. Burning a small piece of paper with intentions written on it is often an effective way to "seal" magical work.

In the next section, we'll get more acquainted with each of the Elements, taking a look at their characteristics, magical associations, and effects on our lives. We'll also look at how the Fifth Element— Spirit—works through each of the other four, and by extension, through ourselves.

PART TWO

ELEMENTAL PHILOSOPHY

THE ELEMENTS

There are many different ways to view the Elements and their significance to Wicca and Witchcraft.

First, let's look briefly at the origins of this concept and its influence on contemporary practices, and then explore the Elements individually as physical and spiritual phenomena.

Understanding as much as you can about how each Element influences the human psyche, as well as the wider world, can help you deepen your magical relationships with these essential forces.

THE FOUR CLASSICAL ELEMENTS

The ancient Greeks believed that all matter was made up of one or more of four elements: Earth, Water, Air, and Fire. These were the basic building blocks of life, and nothing physical existed outside of them.

This idea persisted in scientific thought until a few centuries ago, and historians credit it with evolving into the discovery of the chemical elements modern scientists work with today. But the basic idea behind the Classical Elements, as the Greek concept is now called, was not just philosophy or physical science—the Elements also informed the Greeks' medical practices and spiritual traditions.

Of course, the Greeks were not alone—the notion of all things arising from a handful of natural phenomena is also found in ancient Egypt and Babylonia, and forms of the concept exist in Hinduism, Buddhism, and religions within China and Japan.

Eastern systems differ in the number and identification of Elements. Chinese astrology, for example, recognizes Fire, Water, and Earth, leaving out Air, but includes the two key substances of Wood and Metal, which fall under Earth in Western traditions. The Chinese did not view these Elements as different fixed substances, but more as different forms of energy which is always in flux—an idea, as we have seen previously, echoed in much of the new scientific thinking about the basic nature of matter. Ancient Tibetan philosophy mirrors the original Greek system but adds Space as a fifth Element.

THE FIFTH ELEMENT

The Greeks themselves came to add a fifth Element in the form of what they called *aether*, a word that both names a primordial deity of air and translates as "pure air" or "clear sky." Aether was believed to embody the "upper air," or the air that the gods breathed in the celestial sphere. Among philosophers, Aether was long classified as a type of Air, but Aristotle determined it to be a distinct Element in and of itself, and added it to the list.

This Fifth Element is also widely called *Akasha*, from the Sanskrit word meaning "space." The concept of Akasha appears across many Eastern traditions and is described in one way or another as the original Element from which all creation came, and which still exists in everything and in limitless capacities outside of what we perceive to be the material world.

Later spiritual and religious philosophies would come to associate Akasha with the concept of "Spirit," which is how it is generally defined in Wiccan and Pagan circles.

The Fifth Element is the source and substance of all creation, the invisible unifying force of the Universe, and the conduit through which magic is affected. That it has so many different names and descriptions is perhaps due to its quality of being completely intangible and always mysterious.

ELEMENTAL RELATIONSHIPS

If we take a look at the role the Elements play in ensuring and sustaining life, it's not hard to see why they have been considered the fundamental building blocks of reality.

The human body can be seen as an illustration of this concept, as it makes use of Earth for fuel, Water for substance and sustenance (both in its pure Elemental form and in the form of the blood running through our veins), Fire for the digestive and reproductive processes, and Air for the breath that keeps everything moving. Each Element contributes to our survival, yet each can and does exist entirely independent of us, and of all living beings.

What's just as important as their existence as individual forces, however, is the way they combine and interact to produce the complexity of the world as we know it.

There are several manifestations of the co-creative and interdependent relationships between the Elements. Fire needs Earth and Air to exist, even as it can consume both. And yet, Air can extinguish Fire, depending on the amount and force of each. Water is both absorbed by Earth and able to shape and cover it. Water and Air share the ingredient of oxygen, and each can contain the other. The interrelated qualities of the Elements have powerful potential in spirituality and magic, as in all other areas of life.

THE ELEMENTS AND MODERN OCCULTISM

The influence of the concept of the Elements on Western cultures can be seen in many spiritual and esoteric practices.

While the tradition of alchemy is no longer the popular interest that it was in the Middle Ages, its foundation in the process of transformation using both physical and spiritual means was inspired by the Classical Elements, and has echoes in many modern Pagan traditions. A more widely contemporary Occult tradition with roots in the Middle Ages is the divination system known as the Tarot.

Once used as playing cards in 14th century Europe, Tarot decks grew to be adopted in later centuries as a spiritual tool for accessing information not available on the physical plane. Each card in the Tarot is associated with an Element. In the Minor Arcana, the Elements determined according to the four suits:

Suit	Element
Wands	Fire
Coins	Earth
Cups	Water
Swords	Air

Each suit has associated meanings that correlate to the properties of that Element, which can be used to gain insights into a given Tarot reading. For example, the cards in the suit of Air will pertain to issues of intellect and outlook, decision-making and mental struggles. Many Swords in a given reading may indicate that the questioner is struggling with a conflict or negative attitude, or simply needs to look more closely at a situation.

Undoubtedly though, astrology can take the most credit for keeping an awareness of the Elements alive in popular culture.

Each sign in the wheel of the Zodiac is associated with a specific Element, and astrology holds that our personal characters are shaped not only by the arrangement of the planets at the time of our birth, but also by the qualities of the Element associated with our Sun sign.

Scorpios, for example, tend to be strongly affected by emotions and introspective, though they can be outwardly quite direct and intense in their projection of energy. The other Water signs, Pisces and Cancer, are also more under the pull of their emotions than Earth or Air, but can be more compassionate than Scorpio in the way they relate to others. The Earth signs—Capricorn, Taurus and Virgo—are more grounded and practical than Water signs. Aquarius, Gemini, and Libra, associated with Air, are more detached and can seem unemotional, while Fire signs—Aries, Leo, and Sagittarius—tend toward enthusiasm and impatience.

ELEMENTS AND PERSONALITIES

There's much to learn from the connection with astrology when it comes to how the Elements affect us as people.

While every person is a unique individual, and no two personalities will ever be exactly alike, some broad generalizations can be made about the dominant characteristics of people based on the Element associated with their Sun sign—their dominant Element. *Note, a Sun sign is also referred to as a Star sign or Zodiac sign.*

These characteristics include both positive and negative traits, and each Element comes with its own strengths and challenges. Knowing our dominant Element can help us see ourselves, our individual approaches to life, and our way of interacting with others from a more objective viewpoint. This can help us learn to balance the traits that are not useful in our lives.

If you don't know your Sun sign and thus don't know your Element, it's a good idea to find it by looking up your birthday on the wheel of the Zodiac, or in the table at the end of this book. As you read these introductions to the Elements, their fundamental qualities, and their implications for the human psyche, make note of what you recognize in yourself, as well as what you don't identify with.

You will likely resonate with your dominant Element, but most people find that qualities of other Elements describe them accurately as well. This is because our Sun signs are only one aspect of our makeup according to astrology. Knowing your Moon and Rising signs can offer additional insight into your personality from an Elemental point of view. For example, you might have all three signs in Fire, or have every Element but Earth represented.

Many people find that the Element(s) they're missing in terms of these three aspects of their birth chart corresponds to qualities they struggle to balance. If you seem *not* to be described at all by a particular Elemental description below, you may be missing that Element in your chart!

EARTH

The Element of Earth is probably the most obvious to human perception, since Earth is where we live.

Even those of us in highly urban areas without much access to natural environments are aware that underneath all that pavement is the Earth, without which we would have nowhere to build our houses, roads, and cities.

Earth is, literally, the ground we walk on, as well as where we raise the animals and grow the food we need to survive and thrive. It has also been the source of the clay and minerals with which we've made pottery and cookware to prepare and eat our food, and the trees and stone we've used to build our dwellings.

For the vast majority of human history, the Earth provided everything we needed to survive as a species, with very little in the way of the complex and environmentally damaging processes that go into manufacturing so many of our modern goods. As modern societies, we seem to hold an awareness of this seeming distance from our origins with phrases like "back to the Earth" or "back to the land," used to refer to a felt need to escape the busy, modern city life and spend time in nature.

The idea of being "grounded" is another common metaphor that speaks to the central role Earth plays in our lives. Whether it's a teenager being punished for staying out too late or a busy adult trying to shake off the distractions of the work day through meditation, there's a tradition in modern culture that emphasizes "keeping our feet on the ground" in order to navigate this life successfully. Earth is certainly the most "grounding" of the Elements, with its stable, heavy, passive energy and calming effect.

As a physical reality in and of itself, Earth mostly appears to be unmoving. As such, Earth is associated with the qualities of patience, endurance, and permanence. However, we do see movement in the animals that roam the Earth and, at somewhat slower paces, in the growth of plant life. This connection to growth brings the qualities of diligence and commitment, and the ability to reap what one sows.

Earth personalities

People with Earth as their dominant Element tend to be practically-minded, and are considered to be "sensible" by their peers.

Oriented to the physical manifestations of reality as we know it, Earth people tend to place emphasis on what can be proven through the experience of the five senses, rather than on more subtle, less easily-perceived phenomena. They tend to be reliable, productive, and disciplined, with an innate sense for the workings of the material world and a methodical approach to work that enables them to achieve material security with greater ease than other Elemental personalities. They value stable and long-term friendships and make for honest and kind friends.

The challenge for Earth people is to not let their practicality and desire for structure to keep them from discovering and reveling in life's mysteries, or accessing their own emotional states. Too much Earth energy can lead to becoming rigid or narrow-minded, actually limiting our potential for growth by closing ourselves off to higher-frequency energies that inspire us with new perspectives and motivate us to set our sights on new horizons. People who are described as being "stubborn as a rock" or behaving like "a stick in the mud" are probably exhibiting an excess of Earth energy, and would benefit from loosening up and allowing themselves more access to mystery and joy. They may not always realize that security is, like everything else, ultimately impermanent, that growth is cyclical, and that there are always unseen forces which we may not be able to control, but can make an effort to better understand.

Even the most sensible habits and patterns of living can become overly rigid, and without a certain amount of flexibility it can be hard to navigate the occasional interference that life throws our way. The Earth itself manifests the inevitability of disruption in the form of earthquakes, a phenomenon echoed in the phrase "shaken up" to describe how we feel when unexpected events wreak havoc on the seeming predictability of our daily lives. "Uprooted" is another Earth-related metaphor for how we experience moving from a place we've called home or changing jobs. We are, as human beings, oriented to the ground, and it can be difficult for those with Earth as their dominant energy to feel comfortable in the face of dynamic change.

Ways of connecting with Earth

The Element of Earth is physically represented by the land itself, and all natural forms existing within it and on it.

Trees and forests, rocks and caves, fields and groves are all associated with Earth, and spending time in places that have one or more of these features is a great way to connect with the Earth Element.

Plunge your hands into fresh soil in a garden, walk barefoot in the mud or the grass, or climb a giant boulder and sit on it, feeling its energy resonate with yours. Lie down under the shelter of a leafy tree and feel the ground beneath you supporting your weight, keeping you stable and secure. Place the palm of your hand gently against the trunk of the tree and hold it there for a few moments. Notice its calming effect on your body and thank the tree for its nourishing and sheltering existence.

If you can't get outside, you can practice attuning to Earth energy with a single house plant. Gently touch the soil and the leaves and thank the plant for keeping you company. Spend time noticing and appreciating of the Earth's bounty that you bring home from the grocery store. Hold a potato or other root vegetable in your hands and smell the earthy scents. Doing this before preparing a meal can add much love, intention, and quality to your dinner! Be sure not to take Earth for granted, as it is the foundation of your existence and the ultimate source of all of your abundance.

AIR

In contrast to the visibility of Earth, Air is the Element that we cannot really see at all.

We experience it mostly through our tactile and audial senses, feeling the strength and temperature of a breeze, or hearing the howl of the wind during a storm. Of course, we are in constant interaction with Air via the breath, even though most of the time we're not conscious of it. In fact, you might say Air is the Element we notice the least, unless and until we don't have enough of it!

Air is a traveling energy, not limited to the ground-level perspective of Earth inhabitants, but free to rise and move over great distances. Air inhabits vast realms we have no access to, though recently we've been able to glimpse Air's domain via planes, helicopters, and space shuttles. Because its light density renders it relatively "immune" to gravity, the energy of Air is detached and instantly changeable. Though its quality can be tempered by the presence of the other Elements, Air cannot ever be truly contained.

Air carries sounds and scents from nearby locations, and so informs us about our surrounding environments. We also communicate by pushing air through the lungs and throat in order to speak or sing. Air energy is therefore associated with the qualities of intellect, mental clarity, and communication, and represents the source of knowledge and ideas. It is also the Element of imagination and inspiration—indeed, we speak both literally and figuratively of "needing fresh air" when our indoor environments, or our lives, have become stagnant. We also talk of surprises as coming "out of thin air" or "out of the blue," as if to recognize the link between the invisible forces that influence our lives and the air itself.

Air personalities

People with Air personalities tend to enjoy a higher degree of emotional detachment and objectivity than those with other dominant Elements.

Their "bird's eye view" on life can help them see patterns and possibilities that others can't, and thus avoid the pitfalls of short-sightedness or "stuckness" that people with other personalities might struggle with. Air people tend to have very active minds and feel at home in the realms of abstract thought. They have a knack for discovering new ideas. They are socially energetic and take an interest in the ideas of others, but their dynamic nature and need for movement and free expression may keep them from hanging around in one place for any length of time. They don't want to miss anything by being away too long from their regular, broad-perspectived perch.

The challenge for Air people, then, is to balance their flightiest, high-level energies with more grounded, fixed energies, or else all of that intellectual potential may stay unmanifested in the material world. Just as having one's "feet on the ground" is considered a positive attribute, we tend to speak of having one's "head in the clouds" as something to avoid, at least for too much of the time. "Flighty" is another descriptive word with less-than-positive connotations to describe people who seem to lack focus or substance. Air people need to learn to appreciate the value in being still, as well as being in touch with their emotions, which can often be an uncomfortable realm for them. Getting regular exercise can help them move some of that mental energy to the rest of the body, creating a balance that allows those Air qualities to manifest in more grounded ways.

Ways of connecting with Air

The simplest, most instantly available method for attuning to the energies of Air is through conscious attention to our breath. There are many different meditative breathing exercises, practiced in a range of spiritual and healing traditions, that are worth exploring for their many health benefits. But you can also simply sit with your eyes closed and notice how it feels to breathe.

Another way to spend some time with Air is to watch how individual leaves on a tree interact with the breeze. Anyone who has paid attention knows that leaves and branches don't all move uniformly in response to the push of wind—although in particularly strong winds, this may appear to be the case. Most of the time, if you watch closely, some branches will bend lower than others, and some leaves will flip and flutter much more vigorously than others. Observed in this way, the unpredictable intricacies of Air's movements can be fascinating.

Simply focusing your attention on how Air feels on your skin can be reenergizing, particularly on a hot day when a cool breeze comes sweeping in, even for just a moment. Burning incense is another potential way to bring the positive qualities of Air into your awareness. If you're lucky enough to live in an area that offers views from high elevations, spending some time in such places is great for refreshing your perspective. Mountain locations are ideal for this kind of communing with the Air Element, but rooftops, particularly on tall buildings, can also work wonders. Finally, resurrect that childhood habit of looking for shapes in the passing clouds. (If you never did that as a child, make up for it by starting now!) Notice the pace at which the clouds are moving, whether crawling or racing across the sky, and how their shapes are in constant flux, even when they appear to be relatively still. Cloud-gazing can, with practice and intention, become a powerful method of divination for those able and willing to receive information in this way.

Even when the wind blows hard enough to cause inconvenience, and even though temperatures may be too hot or cold for your liking, be sure to appreciate and thank the Element of Air for its effortless availability in sustaining your life.

FIRE

Fire is probably the most attention-grabbing of all the Elements, due as much to its mesmerizing appearance as to its inherent dangers.

While early humans did live without the use of fire for millennia, the discovery of how to create and control it was essential to our evolution as a species. Fire has allowed us to work and play after sundown, cook nutritious meals, and live comfortably in colder climates. Though its ability to consume nearly everything in its reach makes it a potentially deadly Element, it is this quality that also turns raw metals into tools for easier living.

Fire is different from the other Elements in that it must have another Element to consume in order to maintain its existence, and so is constantly at the work of transformation, and always in motion. It is also the Element of illumination, both for its ability to shed light in the dark, and its association with the Sun.

The energy of Fire is associated with passion—physical and spiritual—as well as strength, willpower, courage, and initiative. We see this demonstrated in the phrase "on fire," used often in amorous contexts, as well as being "fired up" about something one feels to be important, whether a political opinion or a sports team. We also might speak of "feeling the heat" of a stressful or pressurized situation or "putting the heat on" someone in order to get something we want. Fire is also associated with creativity, an energy that lights us up from the inside, as well as the ego, which we sometimes need to watch in order to not let our own thinking get out of control. It is the most active and animated of the Elements, and its power is something we all need to learn to recognize at an early point in our lives, lest we get burned for playing with it.

Fire personalities

People with Fire as their dominant Element tend to command the attention of others. They are generally enthusiastic, vigorous, impassioned, and easily excitable. They make for natural leaders, since they are naturally courageous and willing to charge forth, and they often feel passionate enough about causes or goals that nothing gets in the way of their drive to succeed.

Others are drawn to the light Fire people radiate from the center of their beings. They are often joyful people, and others may feel "lighter" just for being around them. Fire people don't tire easily and tend not to be comfortable sitting still for very long. This is energy that can't be truly contained without extinguishing it.

Of course, just as the Element can be dangerous when not carefully managed, the personality of Fire can get to be too much for others. Fire people may sometimes go overboard in expressing their desires or opinions, or be unaware of the need to "share the floor" during conversations. They can be impulsive and somewhat insensitive compared to other Elemental personalities. They may struggle with a perceived need for immediate gratification or have the tendency to be in a hurry all the time. Too much Fire energy can make a person quick-tempered or even prone to rage, and courage untempered by reason and realism can end up *backfiring*—another word that demonstrates our appreciation for the power of fire.

A balanced approach to living as a Fire person involves learning to ease up on the fuel when appropriate, taking a more long-range view of what will be needed to sustain that energy beyond the present moment. In the days before electricity, households would "bank" their indoor fire overnight, allowing the embers to stay just hot enough to keep it intact for the next morning. Fire people can remember that slowing down and cooling off does not have to mean being extinguished, but can instead be a wise way to ensure success in the long run.

Ways of connecting with Fire

Fire is the one Element that we can't touch with our bodies without potentially serious damage, including death.

Therefore, attuning to its energy is, in the most immediate sense, a "hands-off" activity. However, interacting with Fire is intense, illuminating, and exhilarating all the same, and one can be just as immersed in its energy as in any of the other Elements. Gazing into the flame of a candle is a wonderful, simple way to take in the power of Fire, and a bonfire is even better, especially on a cool, crisp evening when the warmth of the fire adds an extra layer to its magical quality. A fire enjoyed by friends, families, and/or lovers is one manifestation of the love energy this Element brings, as well as its ability to strengthen bonds with others.

Like clouds, flames can make for excellent divinatory communication, as images may appear either in the fire itself, or the smoke as it twists and curls up toward the sky. Crackling embers and the small bursts of energy they release can also be interpreted as messages from the spirit world, and there are even several methods for divination using the ashes from ritual fires.

Moving the body with vigorous exercise and dance is another way to tap into Fire, stoking the heat of our internal "engines" to match the high frequency and vitality of this Element. This way of attuning has the added benefits of building up strength and clearing toxins and other unwanted energy forms from the body. Spending time outdoors in the Sun is also important, and can be extra magical after a long spell of rain or cold Winter weather. Even though the Sun is technically composed of gas, rather than Fire, the two have always been linked together. After all, the Sun does have the ability to burn our skin, and it can certainly start a fire under the right circumstances!

In many traditions, blowing out a candle is considered disrespectful to the spirit of Fire, and people will wave their hands over the flame to put it out instead, or use candle snuffers as a gentler, more attentive method. Whether you adhere to this idea or not, always be respectful of and grateful for the gift of Fire.

WATER

Water shares with Air the ability to move easily, and is the shape-shifter of the Elements. Also like Air, it inhabits physical realms we can't access, in the form of the deepest depths of the oceans and the glacier-covered extremes of the North and South poles.

Water covers most of the planet and manifests in a dizzying array of forms, from the smallest raindrop to an unfathomable tsunami. Essential to the makeup and survival of all living things, Water is nourishing and often soothing, provided we're not tumbling in the rough surf of the ocean or getting drenched in a torrential rain storm!

Water can be completely still or in constant motion, can appear to disappear completely as it joins with Air, and can change to solid form. Its ability to exist in three different states of matter is a testament to the mutability and flexibility of Water. Water will always take the shape of whatever contains it, be it a cup, a pipe, or a depression in a rock. Indeed, it always follows the path of least resistance, as seen when rivers create new pathways in the Earth to get around physical obstacles. Water is powerful—it can flood dry land, extinguish Fire, and when combined with Air can it even dissolve metal over time—but it is also cleansing and purifying.

Water's ability to flow connects it to the realm of human emotions, demonstrated most physically by tears of sadness and joy. The phrase "welling up" is sometimes used to describe a sudden onset of tears caused by emotion. Water is also associated with psychic abilities, as is the Moon, which links to Water through the push and pull of ocean tides. Sensitivity and intuition are related qualities of Water, as are romanticism, generosity, and empathy.

Water personalities

People with Water as a dominant Element are the most naturally psychic of all the Elemental personalities.

Even if they don't realize the source of their intuition and intense feeling, they can be incredibly sensitive to the moods and energies of others, whether those people are in the same room, or, in the case of those they're emotionally close to, very far away on the physical plane.

Water people tend to have a deep understanding of the makeup and motives of the human psyche, and make for good healers and listeners. They are generally creative types, with mystical leanings and an appreciation for the sensual. The energy of Water allows them to be more at home in their emotions than others, which is essentially a prerequisite to being an artist of any kind. Water people love to be in love, and are immersed in the connections they form with others.

The challenges of carrying Water energy include intense emotionality and difficulty maintaining psychic boundaries.

Water people can be overly sensitive, to the point that they are essentially immobilized by all of the stimuli around them and risk drowning in other people's emotions and energies. Depression can be a recurring issue for Water people, as can obsession with wanting to know the unknown before such knowing is possible. Indeed, a drawback of the high levels of psychic activity in Water is that they get accustomed to accessing information unavailable through the usual five senses, and they can get stuck seeking answers to questions they just aren't meant to have answered at the time. They may also unintentionally give away too much of their power to negative people who feed off their kindness and loving natures, and thus become drains on the energies of others.

Some natural Water bodies are stagnant, which, while beneficial for some life forms, is unhealthy for humans to drink. Likewise, Water people can succumb to laziness and lethargy if their energy frequencies are too low. Earth energy is a good starting point for Water people who need balance, as the ground can absorb excess Water. Fire, Water's opposite, can shed light into the shadows, raise the frequency, and brighten the mood.

Ways of connecting with Water

Probably the most powerful way to attune to the energies of Water is to immerse yourself in it.

Swimming in any natural body—ocean, lake, river or pond—is an ideal experience of communion with nature, but this can be a far-away or even unattainable luxury for many people. A pool can also do the trick, as can a relaxing soak in the bathtub. The next time you're immersed in Water, notice the feel of it on your skin and the difference in the way it feels to move your body.

Of course, it isn't strictly necessary to be completely immersed in Water to be in tune with its energy. Dipping a toe or a foot into a stream, taking a refreshing shower, or even running your hand through a bowl of water also forms a direct connection, as does appreciating a long, cold drink of water to quench a thirst.

Water is also experienced through sight and sound—walking along a river or spending time on the beach gazing out at the waves is calming to the body, as is the sound of rain or small waves quietly lapping a shoreline or a river bank. Even recordings of water sounds can help bring people more in touch with their inner selves! As mentioned previously, the calm surface of a bowl of water or even a pond or lake can be used for scrying—Water can speak to you through images, just like clouds and fire. Wherever you encounter Water, be in gratitude for its healing, cleansing, purifying, and nourishing qualities. Allow it to help you open up to the unseen and mysterious forces at work in the Universe—both in yourself and in those around you.

ELEMENTS
AND THE OCCULT

While the Elements are found throughout the natural world, it is not *only* natural features, such as ponds or trees, that represent them in Wiccan and other pagan belief systems.

Ancient cosmologies often held particular gods and goddesses to be associated with one or more of the Elements (such as Vulcan, the Roman god of Fire, from whose name we get "volcano"), and Wicca has continued that tradition.

Other, "lesser" beings are also believed to inhabit the Elements, and these are seen in folklore from across the globe. Some of these entities are less suitable for a Witch's purposes than others—goblins, for example, are generally thought to be mischievous and ill-willed, while other Earth spirits, such as the Greek dryads, are of a more positive persuasion.

Finally, each Element has many associated animals that embody the spirit energy of Earth, Air, Fire, and Water. Wiccans and other Witches may work with deities, Elemental beings, and/or animals as representations of the Elements in their individual spiritual practices.

ELEMENTS AND DEITIES

For those whose belief systems include specific deities, there are many gods and goddesses from cultures around the world who are associated with individual Elements.

Working with these deities in ritual and magic can strengthen your alignment with the Elements, whether you are focusing specifically on magic associated with one particular Element or all of them. It's worth doing some research to discover deities who resonate with you personally, by reading the myths and stories around them and connecting with the cultures they originate in, but here are a few brief examples.

Earth deities include the Greek goddess Demeter, also known as Ceres in the Roman cosmology. She is the goddess of fertility and agriculture, specifically of crops that are processed into edible grains. In fact, the name "Ceres" is the root of the word "cereal," which demonstrates how our modern culture is still connected to ancient beliefs. Ceres was often depicted with a garland of wheat and a basket of fruit and flowers. The god Cernunnos, worshipped throughout Celtic Europe, is also associated with Earth. He is the god of animals, as well as forests and vegetation, and is seen in Paleolithic cave paintings in the form of a stag. He is considered the oldest of the gods in the Celtic pantheon, born of the original mother goddess.

The Egyptian Nut (pronounced "Noot") was the goddess of the sky and the heavens, and so she makes for a good deity to work with in Air magic. Her name is often translated to mean "sky," and, like Cernunnos, she is also a very old deity, found in the creation story of the ancient city of Heliopolis. She was often rendered as a blue-skinned, star-covered woman, arching over the Earth on hands and feet. The widely-known god Thoth is also often associated with Air, as he is credited with inventing writing in the form of hieroglyphs, as well as magic, science, astronomy, and a host of other intellectual pursuits.

In the realm of Fire, the Greek Prometheus plays a crucial role in the origins and development of humankind. He was tasked by Zeus to create the first man from Water and Earth, and then of his own accord he gave humans the power of Fire by stealing it from Zeus' lightning. Brigid, a central figure in the Celtic pantheon and the Irish pantheon in particular, is associated with Fire as the goddess of healing and smithcraft—the art of forging metal over flame. She is said to rule over the "fires" of inspiration, the forge, and the hearth, and sacred flames were kept continually burning in her honor, in some places into the 13th century.

Because the Element of Water is fluid and shape-shifting, existing in such a wide variety of forms, straightforward associations between Water and particular deities are a little more difficult to identify. Many "lesser" deities are associated with specific locations such as rivers and springs, and some of the crone goddesses and underworld gods have Water associations, but deities specifically linked to the Element of Water don't appear with as much frequency as those of the other Elements. Nonetheless, we still find a pair of ancient Sumerian deities—Enki and Nammu—credited with the origins of the world through their associations with Water. Nammu was the goddess of the primordial sea who gave birth to heaven and earth. Enki, born from the air and the earth, was the god of groundwater, or the "freshwater sea" that Sumerians believed existed under the Earth, and was said to have first filled the empty riverbeds with water.

These are just a few examples of deities you might seek relationships with in your exploration of the Elements.

They are given in gender pairs to show possibilities for incorporating both female and male deities—the Goddess and God of the Old Religion—with an emphasis on one or more Elements.

You may feel called by a particular goddess or god, or even by a particular Element—if so, that's a definite sign that you would benefit from pursuing spiritual study in that direction. As always, you should follow your own path and go with your own instincts.

ELEMENTAL BEINGS

Many Pagan and Wiccan traditions also believe in what are usually called "Elementals," or "Elemental Beings."

These are the spirits of Earth, Air, Fire, and Water, and they harken back to the animistic world view of the ancients. These spirits have many names, take many forms, and are the subjects of centuries of legend and lore. Wiccans and Witches who work with Elementals will attest to their presence in nature and in magical ritual.

These beings are said mostly to be unseen, although some particularly sensitive people have seen glimpses of them. Keeping an open mind and a willingness to learn and discover can help you learn to contact and sense them, and ask for their help in your magical workings.

Earth Elementals are widely identified as "gnomes" (meaning "Earth dwellers") in the Western world, although they are also known as "elves," "trolls," and even "faeries." (Some consider faeries to be Air

Elementals, but others, such as the Irish, refer to the spirits of the Earth as faeries.)

These spirits can inhabit a variety of natural features in a given landscape, but are most commonly associated with wooded areas, rocks, caves, and earthen mounds. Spending time in a quiet, undisturbed outdoor area is a good way to start working to connect with Earth spirits. Because of Earth's connection with prosperity and material abundance, leaving offerings like sparkling stones can encourage a relationship with these spirits to flourish.

Working with Earth Elementals in magic is appropriate for spells related to prosperity and success, as well as helping balance negative tendencies toward manipulation and greed. Earth spirits are also helpful in instilling the basic tenacity required to build gradual and long-term abundance, by increasing confidence, practicality, and consistency, as well as a more skillful balance of ambition, caution, and patience.

Air Elementals are most commonly referred to as "sylphs," but, as mentioned above, may also be likened to winged faeries.

They are considered to be present in the clouds, in blowing wind, and other weather phenomena like heavy storms of rain or snow, and were believed in ancient cultures to bring divinatory messages to those able to listen. These spirits of Air are light in energy and quick-moving, so connections with them may have a more fleeting quality than those with Earth spirits, but they also may be felt more tangibly.

It's easier to commune with Air spirits on a breezy or windy day than in very still conditions, but, being of the Air, they are all around us nonetheless. Whistling and/or singing can help one attune with Air Elementals, as can paying attention to any flying insects in the vicinity. It also helps to leave offerings of flowers, which these spirits are said to love.

In magic, Air spirits are helpful for work involving the intellect and communication, developing finer sensitivities to the invisible realms, and responding skillfully to change. As they are also associated with music, they can be called upon to help harmonize disruptive circumstances or relationships.

Fire Elementals are known as "salamanders," perhaps because to those who can perceive them visually: they look like small lizards with tongues of flame, although others see them as tiny balls of light.

These spirits live in all forms of flame, lightning, and the heat of the Sun, and are said to be the catalysts that make the existence of Fire possible.

They are considered by many to be the most powerful of the Elemental beings, and can be fairly easily summoned with the lighting of a candle or building of a fire. Burning incense or sage is a good way to honor and thank them for their presence.

Fire spirits can aid in transformative magic, helping us to see what needs to be eliminated from our lives in order to make room for new growth. Spells for courage, passion, and extra energy are in Fire's domain, both on physical and spiritual levels. Just as the physical manifestation of Fire is potentially dangerous, it's important to respect the power of the spirits of Fire, and not be reckless or excessive with their energies.

Water Elementals are most commonly referred to as "undines," but have also been represented as water nymphs and mermaids in Western traditions.

Existing in all forms of water, these spirits are most commonly associated with rivers, lakes, oceans, springs, wells, and waterfalls.

Spending time near a natural body of water is the most ideal way to connect with Water spirits, who may acknowledge your presence with bubbles or subtle ripples in an otherwise calm surface. Rainy days can also be good occasions for communing with these Elementals. Of course, you can also gaze into the water in a bowl or cauldron.

They are said to appreciate essential oils as offerings, but be sparing with any substance you pour into a natural body of water, and be sure that it's entirely nontoxic to any marine life.

Water spirits are helpful in magic related to love, creativity, and healing, as well as balancing extreme emotions. They help us get in touch with our inner feelings and become more flexible in our approach to solving problems.

People who are new to the Craft sometimes have difficulty taking the concept of Elemental beings seriously.

This is partly due to the way Elementals have been portrayed in our modern, commercialized culture, via Disney movies and Halloween costumes, but it may also be that these spirits are simply not part of one's individual experience of nature. Whether or not you perceive the energies of the Elements as having distinct names and forms, musing on these legendary beings can provide a way into a deeper relationship with the Elements themselves.

As you put more intention into your observance of the natural world, they may just show up for you—as the appearance of faces in trees, a sudden breeze, or dancing shadows around the fire.

ANIMALS
AND THE ELEMENTS

Of course, there is another kind of "Elemental being" which is far more tangible on our plane of existence: every living creature in the animal kingdom.

Animals have played important roles in myth, legend, and spirituality in traditions throughout the world, and are considered sacred by many Witches and Wiccans.

Some Witches work with animal "familiars," which may be physical creatures actually living in their environments, or psychic connections with one or more animals on a purely spiritual level. Others may discover and work with what they describe as "power" or "totem" animals, borrowing from Native American and other shamanic traditions.

In many Wiccan traditions, each of the Elements is associated with a variety of specific animals. Usually, these correspondences relate to habitat—so that most birds are considered Air animals, most sea creatures are Water animals, etc. But habitat is only one source of association. Myths, legends, and characteristics of the animal in question also come into play, particularly when it comes to the animals of Fire.

For example, the lion has long been associated with solar deities, and embodies the qualities of strength, courage, and intensity. Therefore, the lion belongs to the Element of Fire. So does the red fox, associated with passion and desire, and known for its ability to think quickly and change course with agility. The praying mantis is another Fire animal, credited with creating fire among the San people of the Kalahari Desert. The mantis' capacity for both stillness and swift, destructive action is also a source of this association.

Earth animals include the wolf, known for its loyalty and generosity among its own kind; the bear, symbolizing both tranquility and great power; and even the ant, which uses its industrious and determined nature to build its home literally out of the Earth.

Two obvious Air animals are the raven, associated with eloquence and self-knowledge, and the hummingbird, which reminds us of the importance of agility and playfulness. A less obvious correspondence with Air is the spider, which does not fly but spends much of its time suspended above the ground, and is associated with divine inspiration.

Water animals include the dolphin, seen by the ancient Celts as "the watcher of the waters" and associated with playfulness and transcendence; the turtle, able to navigate both land and sea and so associated with adaptability as well as endurance;

and the swan, seen as symbolic of grace and elegance.

Often, the sudden or recurring appearance of an animal in one's life is thought to be a message from the spirit world.

You don't have to be a Witch or a shaman for this to happen in your life. If a particular animal keeps crossing your path, whether literally or in the form of dreams or other seemingly significant references, it can be beneficial to do some research regarding the animal's esoteric meanings, including its associated Element.

You may be being asked to learn something new about yourself, or pay attention to an area of your life that you've been neglecting. As living, breathing embodiments of the Universal life force, animals have much in common with us, and much to teach us about the unseen realms of our magical existence.

REVISITING
THE FIFTH ELEMENT

Having looked closer at each of the Elements that formed the original Classical system and their relationship to many aspects of the Old Religion, it's important to take another look at the Fifth Element—Akasha, or Spirit.

Of course, Spirit is not like the other Elements: it is completely intangible. Unlike the other four, it doesn't exist in its own form separate from anything else.

In a way, Spirit is very much like the sixth sense, which is different from the five senses that are rooted in the physiological processes of the body and therefore not always recognized as a sense. Regardless of their invisibility, Witches know that both Spirit and the sixth sense are very real, and it is often said that the sixth sense is the channel through which Spirit communicates with us. The sixth sense is essential to magic, just as the Fifth Element is essential to all of existence.

Another way of understanding the relationship between Spirit and the four tangible Elements is to look at the sacred meanings of numbers.

Various systems of numerology, dating back to ancient times, recognize the inherent magical qualities of individual numbers and their significance to all of creation. Wiccan and other Pagan traditions clearly value certain numbers—such as three, as reflected in the various triple deities, and thirteen, considered by many to be the ideal number of members in a coven. Two is represented in the male and female deities and the honoring of the night and the day.

The number four is particularly well-represented in the Wiccan belief system. There are four solar holidays in the Wheel of the Year—the equinoxes and solstices—as well as four Earth festivals: Imbolc, Beltane, Lughnasa, and Samhain. There are four main seasons, and four cardinal directions, from which four winds blow. And there are also those four suits, with their corresponding Elements, in the Minor Arcana of the Tarot.

Furthermore, many Wiccan and Pagan traditions connect each of the four tangible Elements to one of the cardinal directions, aligning two sets of four in a beautiful symmetry. This correspondence is enacted in spiritual and magical ritual, as we will see in the next section of this guide.

The alignment of the tangible Elements with these other occurrences of four is one reason why it doesn't make sense to try to "squeeze in" Spirit as a phenomenon in the same category. Instead, Spirit is already in each of the four, as it is in everything we can experience with our six senses, and in everything beyond that.

But there's another aspect of the sacred meaning of numbers—specifically, the number four and the number five—that mirrors the function of the Elements as building blocks in the process of all creation.

In numerological symbolism, the number one represents that which is about to form or take shape—it's the initial idea, thought, inspiration that leads to manifestation, and represents the male aspect of creation. Two, building on one, is the stage of gestation, as the idea takes root and begins to grow. Two is the female aspect. Three is the synthesis of inspiration and growth, and represents the expression of the completed idea, while four is viewed as the physical manifestation—the bringing forth of the idea into material form. The four Elements, seen as the original building blocks of the material world, are the physical manifestations of the original mental energy that created what we know as the Universe.

The number five, then, is essentially what makes new creation possible. It is the necessary catalyst that stirs up the perfect symmetry of the four in order to keep the Universal energy moving—the force that keeps all of creation from being static instead of dynamic. The five is the conduit for manifesting what we desire through magical intention. This number is represented in the pentacle, a major symbol in most Wiccan traditions. The star has five points—one for each tangible Element and one for Spirit. The circle that connects the points pulls all of creation together, and can be said to also represent Spirit, the source of all existence.

Spirit, as the Fifth Element, is what underlies the energy emitted by a crystal, the interaction of a plant with everything visible and invisible in its environment, and the response of water, at the molecular level, to the energies of particular emotions.

It infuses us as living beings, both when we are aware of it and when we are not. When we are aware of Spirit, and when we have clear, positive intentions, we can utilize this basic core energy to manifest desired change in the world. In the next section of this guide, we'll take a more in-depth look at how the magical properties of all five Elements can be channeled to do just that.

PART THREE
ELEMENTAL MAGIC

THE ELEMENTS
IN WICCAN RITUAL

Ritual traditions vary widely, but most followers of the Craft involve the Elements on some level in their practice.

Usually, the Elements are invoked at the start of a ritual—whether it's one of the holidays on the Wheel of the Year, an Esbat (Full Moon celebration), or another occasion, such as an initiation into a coven or any other solitary event of a Witch's choosing.

The Elements are directly invited to participate in the ritual and are appreciated/thanked for their contributions. They may also be asked to assist in some kind of transformational working—a spell, a prayer, a sending of healing energies to a particular person or place. Involving the Elements is a way of connecting with the divine energy as it is expressed in these four distinct forms, allowing us to draw it forth from the incomprehensible source of All That Is into discernible channels.

TOOLS OF WITCHCRAFT

The Elements are usually represented physically on the altar by particular objects that symbolize their individual essences.

These objects are collectively referred to as "tools," though they can also be thought of as something like "ingredients" in the creation of something divine, positive, and timeless. There is quite a variety of tools in the world of Witchcraft, some more elaborate and/or difficult to obtain than others. Those covered here represent a fairly small handful of basic "ingredients" that are particularly relevant to the Elements.

First, a sacred space is necessary. Whether this is a permanent altar or shrine, a "dual-purpose" surface that doubles as a dresser or table, or even a space on the floor, the area where you place your tools and do your work needs to be deliberately chosen and dedicated to the purpose.

Next, you need something to represent each of the Elements. For Earth, a pentacle is great, but a bowl of salt or of earth itself works just as well. For Air, the traditional tool is the wand, which can be made very easily from a small tree branch. Some Witches like to use a bell or a feather instead. Water can be poured into a cup, bowl, or a small cauldron, if you happen to have one. (Alternatively, these can be left empty and still represent Water.) Although candles may be involved in the magical work itself and/or used as lighting, a tea light or other small candle can represent Fire on the altar. Some Witches use an athame, or ritual knife, for Fire.

An alternative is to use crystals or herbs to represent the Elements, which can be a simple and elegant way to connect with the natural world. Specific herbs and crystals associated with individual Elements can be found in the Tables of Correspondence at the end of this guide. If you don't have anything listed here for a particular Element, feel free to use and adapt what you have on hand—be creative! After all, whatever power particular objects may have, it's *you* that charges them, and it's your power fueling whatever transformation you seek.

That being said, it's important to realize that objects *do* have energy, as the animists have always known. Some will be much more energetically resonant than others, and some will feel more pleasant than others.

For example, think about some of your most treasured possessions—perhaps an heirloom passed down from a beloved relative or a work of art you created that you're pleased with. These objects have an energy in their own right, which is tied to how you feel about them, but exists on its own nonetheless.

The same is true of objects you don't feel positive about or attached to. Ever need to get rid of something that belonged to an old love? It's not just about the memories—it's the need to remove that physical energy from your life. Clearing out even your more mundane possessions just "feels good," not only because you've created more space, but because there's less *energetic* clutter, as well.

It is possible to clear an object from negative energy, but it's also true that some tools are just a better energetic fit for a particular person than others. So, again, choose what works best for you. Whatever objects you work with, however, it's important to clear them of all prior energetic imprints before using them in ritual and magic.

Clearing, or "cleansing" a tool can be done in several ways. If the object can get wet, you can start by rinsing it, or wiping it with a clean, dry cloth (it's best to keep a cloth or two just for this purpose, as opposed to something you use for regular housecleaning.) Following this, smudging with sage is a great way to clear energy, but you can also leave the object in sunlight or moonlight for a few hours, or bury it in sea salt, herbs, or soil. Go with your gut, or experiment with different methods to see what works best.

After clearing, it's time to charge the object with your own personal power and positive intention. Consecrating tools can be done with a simple ritual, with or without the more elaborate steps involved on other occasions. Some Witches choose to cast a circle and call the quarters first, while others consider consecration a separate step to be performed before a tool is ever placed on the altar.

Whichever you choose, you can charge the object by holding it over a candle flame (high enough not to burn it, of course!) and/or or lift it up toward the sky. You can also just hold it respectfully in your hands.

Verbalizing the consecration is highly recommended—the power of words goes a long way toward transforming energy, as we saw in the water crystal experiments we discussed in an earlier section. *What* to say is really very much up to you—many Witches prefer to use rhyme and rhythm in their spells, invocations, and other magical work, as this kind of language is considered particularly potent. Others choose their words in favor of being as precise as possible, whether they rhyme or not. You can also simply talk out loud about your intentions as you work to find your own magical voice.

Here's one suggestion for verbalizing the charging of tools:

"Through Earth, Air, Fire, Water and through Spirit, I consecrate this _____ to the Universe and all positive energy, to manifest my intentions with harm to none, and for the good of all."

This can be used with any object for all magical purposes, but if you wish to emphasize a symbolic representation with a particular Element, you might add a phrase or sentence declaring so. For example, *"I consecrate this wand to the Element of Air, and to the Universe..."*

SETTING UP YOUR ALTAR

As with everything else in Witchcraft, the way you set up your altar or sacred space is entirely up to you.

You should go with what feels right and what is visually pleasing for you—if it resonates with you, go with it. You might use a different set-up every time, or you might keep it the same for consistency. ("Ritual" does, after all, tend to involve following an established pattern.)

In terms of focusing on and working with the Elements, it's advisable to place your representations of each Element in its corresponding direction. This means your Earth symbol is in the North, or toward the top of the altar, your Air symbol is in the East (to the right), your Fire symbol is in the South (toward the bottom), and your Water symbol is in the West (to the left).

You may want something in the center to symbolize Spirit and its role in pulling together the other four

Elements. This could be a candle, a quartz crystal, or some other object that is sacred to you.

CASTING THE CIRCLE

It is traditional in Wicca, as well as for other practitioners of the Craft, to cast a magic circle at the start of any ritual.

The circle serves as both a "container" inside which all of the magical energy you are raising will be concentrated, and a "protective boundary" that keeps out any unwanted energy—whether negative or just distracting.

Some Witches cast a circle every time they perform any ritual and/or magical act—even for consecrating tools. Others may save circle-casting for larger, more elaborate rituals such as those used in celebrating Sabbats and Esbats. Still others consider the circle completely optional, and may not cast one at all. This is an individual choice, but casting is recommended for beginners, as it can help you feel the energy you're raising in a more focused way.

There are many ways to cast a circle. You can physically mark the circle with candles, stones, herbs, and/or sea salt beforehand, or allow the circle to remain invisible. Standing inside the circle, point your wand, athame, or index finger to the ground at the circle's northernmost point. Walk clockwise around the circle, continuing to point, and visualize your personal power charging the ground at the circle's edge. You can do this just once, but it can be more effective to walk the circle three times, visualizing the power growing stronger with each rotation. Note: Make sure you have everything you'll need before you take this step, as it's not wise to break the energy of the circle once it's been cast!

CALLING THE QUARTERS

As mentioned above, each of the four Elements is associated with one of the four cardinal directions. When invoking the Elements into ritual, these directions, also called "quarters," serve as physical locations from which to locate and engage the specific energies of each Element.

Once the circle is cast (if you are doing so), the Elements can be invited into the sacred space. This can be a fairly simple step or a more elaborate process, depending on your preferences. Some Witches light a candle for each of the Elements while invoking them with words, and ritual hand gestures, while others may simply silently invite them into their ritual space.

Here is one approach to invoking the Elements that focuses on acknowledging the energetic identity of each. This can be done before any type of ritual, or as a way of starting your day by grounding and centering with the forces of nature. As you speak to each Element, be sure to face its corresponding direction.

Facing North:

"Spirit of Earth,
Welcome to this sacred space.
Thank you for the gifts of stability and abundance,
and for bringing your energy to this moment."

Facing East:

"Spirit of Air,
Welcome to this sacred space.
Thank you for the gifts of knowledge and harmony,
and for bringing your energy to this moment."

Facing South:

"Spirit of Fire,
Welcome to this sacred space.
Thank you for the gifts of passion and transformation,
and for bringing your energy to this moment."

Facing West:

"Spirit of Water,
Welcome to this sacred space.
Thank you for the gifts of intuition and empathy,
and for bringing your energy to this moment."

CLOSING THE RITUAL

Whatever your purpose for ritual—be it a Sabbat or a quick, simple spell—it's important to intentionally close the work and the sacred space before returning to "business as usual" in ordinary reality. (Neglecting to do so can result in feeling somewhat chaotic or "out of sorts," and possibly troubled sleep.)

Once your spiritual work is done, "release" the Elements by thanking them individually, perhaps moving in a counter-clockwise direction as you do so. If you have cast a circle, close it by walking counter-clockwise three times, visualizing any remaining magical energy returning to the ground. Stand quietly for a moment, clearing your mind of the ritual and/or spellwork, knowing that you've sent your power out into the Universe and that your intentions will be manifested in the way and at the time which is best for all.

MAGICAL PERCEPTION

Before we look at specific spells and other magical work, it's important to emphasize that simply following these steps as if following a recipe is unlikely to have any transformational effect.

The focused power of the mind is really where the magic comes from. This can be a challenge for many in this busy, noisy modern world, but developing some kind of meditation practice can strengthen your connection to the divine, and consequently, your magic.

There are many helpful resources out there in this department, including meditations, visualizations, and other mental/spiritual exercises specifically for the practice of Witchcraft. Below are four ways of strengthening your psychic "muscles" for magical work as you deepen your connection with the Elements.

EARTH: TALKING
TO THE PHYSICAL WORLD

As you get up to start your day, and when you return from being out, say hello to your home. Say hello to each room, and to your favorite things in your home, whatever they may be.

This may feel a bit silly at first, but remember that there is Spirit in all things. As you get in the habit of greeting the energy in your home, you will notice that your mood lifts as you do so.

Pay extra attention to your magical and sacred objects—your altar tools, special stones, herbs, etc. Acknowledge the spirit energy in these objects, and thank them for being in your life. You are strengthening an energetic bond between you and these sacred tools that will empower your magical work.

AIR: BREATHWORK
AND VISUALIZATION

A very effective way to ground and center before working magic is through conscious breathing.

Through the breath we can open ourselves more deeply to the Element of Spirit and clear a path for sending our focused intentions out into the Universe. Basic 3-part yogic breathing is an ancient practice that quiets the mind and gets you closer to the state of mind that magical transformation requires.

Lying on your back, focus on breathing in slowly, allowing the air to fill your lower abdomen, then upper abdomen, then all the way to the top of your lungs. When it's time to breathe out, do so in the reverse order, pushing the air from the top of your body out first, and ending with the lower abdomen. (Note: It's best to breathe in and out through your nose, but if you have a cold, don't let that stop you!)

Do this five times, focusing entirely on your breath. Then, allow yourself to breathe normally, as you visualize the result of your intentions manifesting. For example, if you're dealing with money issues, call up the feeling of being completely secure in your finances, with all the bills paid and plenty to spare. Spend some time strengthening this feeling, and hold it as consistently as you can while you perform the magical work.

FIRE: FLAME AND FOCUS

Candles are great for strengthening concentration and psychic power. All you need is a quiet space and a lit candle.

For the first exercise, sit before the flame and gaze into it for a few moments. (Take care of your eyes by training your gaze toward the bottom of the flame, and be sure to blink whenever you need to.) When you're ready, close your eyes, and watch for the image of the flame against your closed eyelids. Hold onto this image for as long as you can before your concentration breaks. When the flame disappears, open your eyes and start again. Over time, you will be able to prolong the flame's appearance in your mind's eye.

Next, practice "shaping" the flame with your own thoughts. As you watch the flame, visualize it growing, shrinking, getting brighter and dimmer. Keep your focus trained on the flame and the change you're visualizing at the same time. You may not see an effect at first, as this takes practice, but after a time you will notice the flame respond to your projections. To strengthen the psychic energy further, be sure you've spoken to your candle and have done some meditative breathing first!

WATER: TRUSTING THE FLOW

This visualization is good for attaining an optimal mind frame for magic.

Start with some meditative breathing. With eyes closed, bring to the "screen" of your mind an image of a pond. The surface of the pond is completely still, reflecting the blue sky above it and the tops of several tall trees around its perimeter. You are standing at its southern shore, feeling the warmth of the Sun on your shoulders. Across the pond, to the North is a particularly large, knotty oak tree. To the East are three robins chattering to each other on the branches of a leafy shrub, and to the West, a stand of cattails and other marsh grasses obscure the pond's shoreline.

Hold this vision in your mind until it's quite solid. Then, visualize a small, round pebble in the palm of your dominant hand. Feel the smooth, cool surface of the pebble between your fingers, and then gently toss it into the center of the pond. Watch and hear the tiny splash it makes before disappearing under the surface. Watch the ripples it creates radiating out from the center in perfect circles. Choose a single small wave to focus on, following it until it travels all the way to the pond's northern shore. Note how the ripples continue to move outward from the center, long after the pebble has settled on the bottom of the pond. This is a good metaphor for magic—the energy of the action continues to change the physical world around it long after the action itself has been performed.

ELEMENTAL
SPELLS AND CHARMS

The following magical workings make use of the energies of the particular Element they are based in. These can be done as part of a larger ritual, or on their own. Be sure to ground and center beforehand, spending time in meditation and focusing on your intention.

Remember to always respect the power of magic, and do your work in the spirit of what is good for all and harms none.

Please note that while the ingredients listed below work well, you are free to make substitutions where necessary or desired. The Tables of Correspondence at the end of this guide provide more information about herbs, oils, and crystals in terms of their Elemental associations, and can be a starting place for finding alternatives.

EARTH SPELLS

Abundance Coins

This is a good charm for attracting extra money from unexpected places.

- 2 coins—matching denominations of your choosing (older coins are nice if you have them, but it doesn't matter.)

- 1 small piece of cloth—a scrap of fabric is fine.

- 1 green ribbon

- 1 tablespoon total dried rosemary, thyme, and/or cinnamon

- Patchouli oil

Lay the herbs on the center of the cloth. Anoint the coins with a drop of the patchouli oil, speaking your intentions aloud as you do so—remember, your words are not particularly important, but rather the intent behind them.

Push the coins gently into the herbs, wrap the cloth over the coins, and tie with the ribbon. Place the coin bundle somewhere in your home where you will see it often, and carry it with you in your pocket or purse when you go out.

Harmony in the Home

To help with interpersonal conflicts or simply
unsettled energy where you live, try this spell, which is
particularly helpful in the weeks before Winter sets in.

- Basil and honeysuckle, roughly one tablespoon of
  each—fresh herbs are preferable, but dried also
  works well.

- 1 dried leaf—if you must pick a leaf from a tree,
  choose from a well-flourishing tree, pick gently,
  thanking the tree, and leave the leaf to dry before
  using.

- Mortar and pestle—if you don't have these, a
  bowl and your fingertips will work fine.

- Cedar or sandalwood incense (optional)

Light the incense, if using. Slowly pour the basil into
the mortar or bowl, saying, *"with this basil, I keep all
negative energy away from my home."* Add the
honeysuckle, saying, *"with this honeysuckle, I bring all
positive energy into my home."* Stir the two herbs
together with the pestle or mix with your fingertips.
Take the leaf and crumble it gently over the herbs,
saying, *"there is harmony in every corner of this
home"* three times. Mix the leaf into the herbs while
concentrating on feeling peaceful, at ease, and secure
in your dwelling.

Sprinkle the mixture around the outside of your home, walking around it in a clockwise circle. If this is not possible, sprinkle it discreetly around as much of the outside area as you can. You can also use potted plants for this step, if necessary.

AIR SPELLS

Four Winds Incantations

The specific direction of the wind can make for an excellent magical tool, depending on your purposes. Try this on a particularly windy day for a stronger connection with the magical energy you're communing with. Be sure to choose an intention aligned with the wind's direction.

- North winds: financial, home, practical matters

- East winds: change, new beginnings, fresh perspective, creativity

- South winds: love, lust, passion, vitality, initiative, courage to follow through

- West winds: healing, cleansing, intuition, emotional concerns

Stand outdoors, facing the wind, with your feet a few inches apart, back straight, head held high, and arms a few inches from your sides with palms outward. (This is a slight modification the yogic "Mountain pose," appropriate here for its aid in aligning your vertical energy from the ground through the crown of your head. Mountains are also associated with the Element of Air.)

Take three deep breaths, place your palms together, and raise your arms to the sky. Verbalize your intention in connection with the wind. You might say, for example, "*In this East wind, I manifest a new way forward in my career, for the good of all, and with harm to none.*" Allow your intention to be carried on the wind. Then, keeping your palms together, slowly bring your hands down in front of your solar plexus. Take another deep breath, and close the ritual in your own way.

Spell for Clarity and Concentration

This is good for tests, projects at work, or anything that requires focus and feels challenging.

- 1 dried dandelion flower (or leaf, if out of season)

- Peppermint oil

- 1 piece of paper

Write the task you're seeking help with on a piece of paper. Rub a drop of the peppermint oil into the paper as you say these words: "*With a sharp, clear, focused mind, I complete this well, in the desired time.*" Scatter the dandelion flowers/leaves over the paper, and leave it on your altar until the task is finished.

FIRE SPELLS

Transforming Through Banishing Old Habits

This spell enacts transformative magic through the physical burning of the representation of what you want to be rid of in your life—whether this is a physical habit or a way of thinking that you want to release.

- 1 small black candle

- 1 small piece of paper

- 1 Fire-proof dish (or sink)

Light the candle. On the paper, either write or draw a symbol of what you are banishing. As you do so, imagine your life without this negative habit, and visualize the joy you will feel when it's gone. When you're ready, say, "*I release this habit of _____, and welcome in the positive energy created by its absence.*" Light the paper with the candle and let it burn out in the fire-proof dish, or in the sink, if necessary. (As with anything fire-related, be very careful with this step!) Leave the candle to burn out on its own in a safe place.

Bringing Love

This can be used to attract love into your life if you're single, or rejuvenate an existing relationship. However, if you struggle with self-love, your best bet is to start there, as you need it to sustain lasting love with someone else. Be very careful not to aim your energy at a specific person in a manipulative way, as this can backfire. In your visualization, you don't concentrate on controlling the feelings of another—instead, concentrate on how *you* want to feel.

- 3 pink candles

- 1 red candle

- Ginger oil

- Rose quartz

Rub ginger oil into the red candle. Place the pink candles on the altar in a triangle, with one to the North, one to the East, and one to the West. Place the red candle in the center of the triangle. Light the pink candles, then hold the rose quartz in both hands with your eyes closed.

Visualize the feeling of being incredibly, unconditionally loved, allowing the feeling to grow as you strengthen your focus. When you're ready, open your eyes, and place the rose quartz just above the North pink candle. State your intention, and light the red candle, visualizing your personal power streaming through the flame and up into the Universe.

WATER SPELLS

Magical Water for Stress Relief

Crystal elixirs* have long been used in magical and healing traditions for a variety of purposes.

Try the simple transformative power of an amethyst elixir to clear away any energetic patterns resulting from built-up stress, resentment, or other negative states of mind. Amethyst calms nerves and strong emotions, relieves tension, and helps rebalance oversensitivity. First, cleanse and charge the amethyst with your specific intention. You can say, "*I clear away all stress/fear/anger regarding _____.*"

Place it in a glass, pour in at least one cup of purified water, and cover. Leave the glass in moonlight or sunlight for at least 4 hours, or longer in cloudy conditions. When it's time to use your elixir, uncover it, state your intention again, and take seven sips. State the intention one more time, and drink most of the remaining water, leaving a little at the bottom of the glass. Dip your index finger into the glass, close your eyes, and trace a circle with the water on your forehead. Take a deep breath. Then, thank the water and the stone for their assistance.

*Before using any other crystal in an elixir, be sure to research it! Many crystals and stones are toxic to the body and should not be placed in drinking water.

Problem-Solving Sleep Spell

Tricky problems and difficult decisions are often a cause of poor sleep. This spell helps hand those worries over to the Universe while we get to the important business of quality rest! Very often, the needed solution or answer will arise the day after this spell is performed, though, depending on the circumstances, it may evolve more slowly.

- Sleep-aiding tea, such as a blend of chamomile, spearmint, and lemongrass—make your own or use a nice commercial blend.

- 1 bowl—glass or ceramic, but not plastic

- 1 cup of water

- Dried lavender or lavender essential oil

- Moonstone or citrine

- 1 white tea light

Make and steep the tea as you do the following:

Hold the moonstone or citrine and focus on your question. (*Don't* focus on what you think may be the possible answers, or dwell on the apparent lack of solutions—simply focus on the question or problem itself.) Place it in the bowl, and pour in the water. Light the tea light. Thank the Universe for all you will learn from the experience of the particular question/problem, as well as for its answer or solution. Sprinkle the lavender oil or herb into the water. Drink the tea while meditating on something positive and unrelated to the problem or question. If the problem/question arises in your mind, keep letting it go, without judgement.

GOING FORWARD

These are just a few suggestions for consciously working with the Elements in your magic. As you develop your Craft, it's best to create your own spells and charms according to your intuition and connection with the Spirit of the Universe. Continue to read widely and always disregard information or suggestions that don't feel right to you. Most importantly, continue to cultivate your energetic relationship with the living world around us.

CONCLUSION

Many people first learn of the Wicca religion in the context of Magic and Witchcraft.

Although there is *far* more to Wicca than Witchcraft, I wanted to create a guide that helped newcomers and seasoned Witches alike to learn about the properties of the Elements that make up our Universe—as well as providing knowledge for readers who want to practice Witchcraft. After all, a great number of Wiccans *do* practice Witchcraft, whether on special occasions such as the Sabbats or as part of their daily routine, and as such, the information is important.

Of course, the way Magic and Witchcraft is portrayed in Hollywood is *very* different from how it is practiced in reality. However, the only thing that really matters is to always practice Witchcraft from a good place, and with good intent—you should never perform spellwork that deliberately seeks to harm another person, or encourages them to act against their will. Love spells are a great example of this, as, although love is a positive emotion, forcing a specific person to fall in love with you is highly manipulative.

This isn't an issue for most Wiccans—our appreciation of nature and the world around us means we are a peaceful bunch! However, for anyone planning on practicing Witchcraft for mischievous ends, the *Threefold Law* is highly ingrained into the Wiccan belief systems. This essentially says that whatever intent you send out into the Universe—in other words, good or bad—will come back to you three times as great. While some Wiccans will disagree over the existence of this cosmic 'law,' it is still a useful guideline to follow, and encourages all of us to be better human beings.

In this guide, I have attempted to take an unbiased approach wherever possible; however, as nothing with Wicca is set in stone, my own experiences as a practicing Wiccan may have influenced certain sections of the book. I have tried to be open and informative about the differing beliefs among Wiccans, and make reference to them where relevant, but some information presented will undoubtedly be influenced by my own journey and understanding of the topics.

To become a practicing Wiccan you do not have to share all of the beliefs I hold, or the ones presented in this guide. If something doesn't *feel* right to you, you're free to find your own path, and incorporate the beliefs and practices that *do* resonate with you. For many Wiccans, their beliefs are constantly changing with every new experience they face. My advice to you is to keep an open mind, as what you believe to be true today could alter a great deal tomorrow.

In my opinion, this is the best thing about Wicca: it is a lifelong journey, on which you will never stop learning!

I will leave you with that thought, though I sincerely hope that this guide to the Elements has given you a better understanding of the Universe and the world you inhabit. I have included a number of tables of correspondence at the end of this guide, which should prove useful as a reference point for any further study of the Elements.

I sincerely hope you enjoyed learning about Wicca and Witchcraft with me, and I would love for you to become a regular practitioner—by following the outlines in Part Three, you have everything you need to get started. However, if this is the end of your Wiccan journey, I hope you have learned something new, and that you better understand the belief system of the wonderful people who practice Wicca.

Thank you one more time for reading.

Blessed Be.

TABLES OF CORRESPONDENCE

These tables of correspondence illustrate various qualities and associations of tangible objects like crystals and stones, herbs, and oils, as well as intangible phenomena like colors, directions, and astrological signs. Included here are tables of correspondence between the Elements and their various associations, including physical objects used to represent them in ritual and magic.

The information here is by no means complete, but is intended as a basic reference as you explore your practice of the Craft through an Elemental lens. Utilizing the tools and "ingredients" listed here can help you strengthen your connection with the Elements, and therefore with the powers of the Universe. Try working with the stones, herbs, tools, etc. that you feel an affinity with, as well as introducing yourself to new ones from time to time.

TABLE ONE: ELEMENTS AND SPIRITUAL ASSOCIATIONS

Elements	Primary Qualities	Magical Purposes	Astrological Signs
Earth	Stability, discipline, prosperity, abundance	Employment, business, money, success in endeavors, fertility	Capricorn, Taurus, Virgo
Air	Intellect, communication, imagination, harmony	Creativity, concentration, inspiration, psychic abilities	Aquarius, Gemini, Libra
Fire	Passion, illumination, transformation, enthusiasm	Joy, love, strength, willpower, resolving anger	Aries, Leo, Sagittarius
Water	Emotion, sensitivity, intuition, empathy	Healing, purification, friendship issues, general well-being	Pisces, Cancer, Scorpio
Spirit	None	All	All

Elements	Cardinal Direction	Season	Animals
Earth	North	Winter	Wolf, bear, ant, bull and cow, horse, deer, dog
Air	East	Spring	Raven, hummingbird, most other birds and winged insects, spider
Fire	South	Summer	Fox, lion, tiger, lizard, praying mantis
Water	West	Autumn	Dolphin, turtle, swan, whale, most other sea animals and sea birds
Spirit	Center	All	All

TABLE TWO: ELEMENTS AND PHYSICAL ASSOCIATIONS

Elements	Ritual Tools	Colors	Crystals and Stones
Earth	Pentacle, bowl of salt or earth	Green	Jade, pyrite, moss agate, tourmaline
Air	Wand, incense, bell, feathers	Yellow	Aventurine, mottled jasper, turquoise, topaz
Fire	Candle, athame, incense	Red	Amber, bloodstone, garnet, tiger's eye
Water	Chalice	Blue	Amethyst, aquamarine, lapis lazuli, moonstone
Spirit	Magic circle, positive intention	Violet, white, black	Jet, onyx, quartz crystal

Elements	Herbs	Essential Oils
Earth	Horehound, moss, mugwort	Cypress, honeysuckle, oakmoss
Air	Red clover, comfrey leaf, dandelion	Frankincense, lemon balm, lavender
Fire	Basil, cayenne, nettles	Bergamot, ginger, rosemary
Water	Catnip, hibiscus flower, passion flower	Lemon, chamomile, sandalwood
Spirit	All, but especially mistletoe	All

SUGGESTIONS FOR FURTHER READING

Please note that this is a very brief list. Many other interesting and useful resources are available in print and online.

Ellen Dugan, *Natural Witchery: Intuitive, Personal & Practical Magick* (2007)

Peter Tompkins and Christopher Bird, *The Secret Life of Plants* (1973)

Masaro Emoto, *Messages From Water and the Universe* (2010)

Itzhak Bentov, *Stalking the Wild Pendulum: On the Mechanics of Consciousness* (1977)

John C. Briggs and F. David Peat, *Looking Glass Universe: The Emerging Science of Wholeness* (1986)

David Rankine and Sorita d'Este, *Practical Elemental Magick: Working the Magick of Air Fire Water & Earth in the Western Esoteric Tradition* (2008)

THREE FREE AUDIOBOOKS PROMOTION

Don't forget, you can now enjoy **three audiobooks completely free of charge** when you start a free 30-day trial with Audible.

If you're new to the Craft, *Wicca Starter Kit* contains three of Lisa's most popular books for beginning Wiccans. You can download it for free at:

www.wiccaliving.com/free-wiccan-audiobooks

Or, if you're wanting to expand your magical skills, check out *Spellbook Starter Kit,* with three collections of spellwork featuring the powerful energies of candles, colors, crystals, mineral stones, and magical herbs. Download over 150 spells for free at:

www.wiccaliving.com/free-spell-audiobooks

Members receive free audiobooks every month, as well as exclusive discounts. And, if you don't want to continue with Audible, just remember to cancel your membership. You won't be charged a cent, and you'll get to keep your books!

Happy listening!

MORE BOOKS BY
LISA CHAMBERLAIN

Wicca for Beginners: A Guide to Wiccan Beliefs, Rituals, Magic, and Witchcraft

Wicca Book of Spells: A Book of Shadows for Wiccans, Witches, and Other Practitioners of Magic

Wicca Herbal Magic: A Beginner's Guide to Practicing Wiccan Herbal Magic, with Simple Herb Spells

Wicca Book of Herbal Spells: A Book of Shadows for Wiccans, Witches, and Other Practitioners of Herbal Magic

Wicca Candle Magic: A Beginner's Guide to Practicing Wiccan Candle Magic, with Simple Candle Spells

Wicca Book of Candle Spells: A Book of Shadows for Wiccans, Witches, and Other Practitioners of Candle Magic

Wicca Crystal Magic: A Beginner's Guide to Practicing Wiccan Crystal Magic, with Simple Crystal Spells

Wicca Book of Crystal Spells: A Book of Shadows for Wiccans, Witches, and Other Practitioners of Crystal Magic

Tarot for Beginners: A Guide to Psychic Tarot Reading, Real Tarot Card Meanings, and Simple Tarot Spreads

Runes for Beginners: A Guide to Reading Runes in Divination, Rune Magic, and the Meaning of the Elder Futhark Runes

Wicca Moon Magic: A Wiccan's Guide and Grimoire for Working Magic with Lunar Energies

Wicca Wheel of the Year Magic: A Beginner's Guide to the Sabbats, with History, Symbolism, Celebration Ideas, and Dedicated Sabbat Spells

Wicca Kitchen Witchery: A Beginner's Guide to Magical Cooking, with Simple Spells and Recipes

Wicca Essential Oils Magic: A Beginner's Guide to Working with Magical Oils, with Simple Recipes and Spells

Wicca Elemental Magic: A Guide to the Elements, Witchcraft, and Magical Spells

Wicca Magical Deities: A Guide to the Wiccan God and Goddess, and Choosing a Deity to Work Magic With

Wicca Living a Magical Life: A Guide to Initiation and Navigating Your Journey in the Craft

Magic and the Law of Attraction: A Witch's Guide to the Magic of Intention, Raising Your Frequency, and Building Your Reality

Wicca Altar and Tools: A Beginner's Guide to Wiccan Altars, Tools for Spellwork, and Casting the Circle

Wicca Finding Your Path: A Beginner's Guide to Wiccan Traditions, Solitary Practitioners, Eclectic Witches, Covens, and Circles

Wicca Book of Shadows: A Beginner's Guide to Keeping Your Own Book of Shadows and the History of Grimoires

Modern Witchcraft and Magic for Beginners: A Guide to Traditional and Contemporary Paths, with Magical Techniques for the Beginner Witch

FREE GIFT REMINDER

Just a reminder that Lisa is giving away an exclusive, free spell book as a thank-you gift to new readers!

Little Book of Spells contains ten spells that are ideal for newcomers to the practice of magic, but are also suitable for any level of experience.

Read it on read on your laptop, phone, tablet, Kindle or Nook device by visiting:

www.wiccaliving.com/bonus

DID YOU ENJOY
WICCA ELEMENTAL MAGIC?

Thanks so much for reading this book! I know there are many great books out there about Wicca, so I really appreciate you choosing this one.

If you enjoyed the book, I have a small favor to ask—would you take a couple of minutes to leave a review for this book on Amazon?

Your feedback will help me to make improvements to this book, and to create even better ones in the future. It will also help me develop new ideas for books on other topics that might be of interest to you. Thanks in advance for your help!